MONEY PATHS

6 REAL WAYS TO MAKE MONEY
AS A NEW LIFE COACH

Discover the pros, cons, real money math, and exactly what you need to do to get started in this simple guide.

TABLE OF CONTENTS

Introduction...9

Option 1: Private Coaching.....................................17

Option 2: Group Coaching 31

Option 3: Retreats 45

Option 4: Writing a Book 57

Option 5: Create a DIY Online Program 67

Option 6: Become an Affiliate
   or Referral Partner 79

Hello!

If you are feeling scared, overwhelmed, or just confused about how to make money as a coach you are in the right place!

Take a deep breath and relax.

We've got you covered now!

How to Use this Guide
(Don't Panic!)

Hello awesome person!

What you have in your hands (or on your screen) is a real, no-holds-barred, overview of 6 very real ways to make money as a life coach.

Or, as I like to call it, the 6 money paths.

My goal with this book, and over at the Coach Pony community, is to help you make an informed, real, down-to-earth decision on how to build your life coaching practice.

Why?

Because if you don't understand the business of coaching, then you'll find it hard to have success as a coach.

And, as much as I'd love to say, "YOU CAN DO EVERYTHING!" *the truth is that you can't.*

Not all money paths will work for you and your lifestyle.

So, let's put down the unicorns and rainbows and focus in on what works and *what doesn't.*

Each section in this book includes:

1. A simple overview of the money path.
2. Pros and cons of each money path.
3. An honest assessment of if you should try it or not.
4. Real money math, so you get an idea of how much income each area can produce
5. A super simple checklist of how to get started, so that you have an idea of what is involved in each path (and don't get overwhelmed before you start!).
6. Helpful tools that you may want to consider using if you take that money path.
7. Some sections will also contain a quick and dirty inside story on how to get started, from my personal experience, so that you have a real-life example of what a money path can look like.

What isn't included:
This is not an exhaustive guide or manual on how to successfully set up your business in each of these money paths. For that, you'll need a deep program like this one, over at www.buildarealbusiness.biz. But it IS enough information for you to get a real idea of what is involved in each path so that you know what will be best for you and your future clients. Yay!

INTRODUCTION

WELCOME.

Welcome to a really great career in a booming industry!

Life coaching continues to expand further into the mainstream, as more companies (and individuals) are realizing how effective it can be to have a professional coach on hand, focused on helping people achieve goals and become an even better version of themselves.

If you aren't a certified life coach, or you haven't explored getting certified, it's useful to check out the International Coaching Federation and look at schools that they have accredited. The certification process is a lot like getting your master's degree... while also going to intense therapy. It's an intensive, and pretty spectacular, personal journey.

But whether you are certified or not, you are probably wondering if you can make any money as a coach, and if so, how to do it! And if you find yourself on a hamster wheel of anxiety, constantly asking yourself "How do I start? What should I do first? What makes the most sense for me? Should I even DO this life coaching thing?" Then I'm here to tell you that you are in exactly the right place to figure it out, and you are *definitely* not alone.

When I started my coaching business 6 years ago after leaving a cushy corporate job, I was a sweaty, stressed-out, nacho-eating mess. I can remember sitting alone on my couch holding onto my computer for dear life, just hoping I'd figure this whole coaching thing out.

Before I became a Forbes Top 100 for careers, or a Top 29 coach to follow, or had over 1,000 paying clients, I was mostly just a combination of afraid and overwhelmed, not knowing how I was actually going to make money and pull off being a full-time coach. There were so many options, and it was all so confusing.

Sound familiar?

You probably have a million ideas in your head, like "I should coach one-on-one!" or "I want to reach

MILLIONS" or "I am ready to group coach" or "I want to write a book! I'm so excited!"

And then...

...you pause.

Which of these is the right path for you?

All?

None?

Where do you even begin?

What are the pitfalls?

What will help you reach your dream business first?

ARGGHHHHHH!

Whew

Let's all take a deep breath for a second because the truth is that you can absolutely figure this out.

All you need is the right information.

(That's where I come in).

I've created online programs, which generate thousands of dollars each month while I sleep.

I've hosted profitable high-end retreats for different career and business groups, allowing me to visit wine country and take my business on vacation while also serving my clients (I should mention I love wine and chocolate!).

I've written a book that has sold thousands of copies, just from my website.

I've created small and large group programs which generate 6+ figures a year, each.

I've done high-end private coaching, and I topped out at charging $6500 per private client with a wait-list to work with me before my business grew too big to coach one-on-one anymore.

And I've been a partner to other coaches, which resulted in me picking up a few thousand dollars from sending a single email.

I share all of this not to brag, but instead to say that I've seen the good, the bad, and the ugly of each up close, and I want to give this hard-earned information to you.

Why? Because you are awesome!

And knowledge is power.

The right knowledge at the right time can save you a tremendous amount of time, money, and stress. And, even more importantly, the right knowledge at the right time can literally make you money.

So, before you hang out your shingle and really do this coaching thing, let's start with how you really truly make money as a coach, so you can find a money path that's right for you.

Because if you can't support yourself, you can't support your clients.

Ready?

Grab some caffeine (or some wine, I'm not choosy) and let's begin!

OPTION 1: PRIVATE COACHING

Private coaching is where most coaches begin, and almost all coaches work.

It's where I started too before I built up all of my programs and automated my business. And the truth is that private coaching was how I made my first 6 figures in business!

But enough about me, let's talk about YOU.

I know you already know what private coaching is, but for giggles let's just review: As a private coach, you exchange money for hours, as you help a client achieve a particular goal.

You work with people one-on-one, and you usually meet with them for a 50 minute or 60-minute sessions regularly for a period of time, often 3-5 months. It can be longer, it can be shorter, but 3-5 months is a good rule of thumb.

You work with your clients on a specific goal, and while you can't make guarantees, you work to help your clients achieve that goal in the time allotted.

You may allow email or other contact in between sessions, but either way, private coaching is a high-level of service that is 100% tailored to your clients.

It's also intensely profitable. Most coaches charge between $1000 and $5000 per package, with some executive coaches reaching $25,000 per package.

So, let's dive in!

The pros of private coaching:
—>*It's instantly profitable,* especially if you keep your overhead costs low (i.e., not renting expensive office space!). If you are signing 3-4 clients a month at $2,000-$4,000 each, then you are making right around six figures annually in your business. Go you!

—>*It requires very little in terms of infrastructure.* The truth is that building and maintaining big program offerings like I run in my business takes effort. Including a lot of tools, time, and people. But to be a private coach you only need a few things, like a simple website or LinkedIn page for your business, a way to take payment like a check or Paypal, and a simple scheduling tool like Calendly,

Acuity, or Schedule Once. These can be fairly easy and inexpensive to set up and should cost you very little out of pocket.

—>*It's a great way to get started and build confidence.* Look, when you are a new coach you are often figuring things out as you go. **You have to do it in order to learn**! And working with folks one-on-one allows for a lot of flexibility along the way – you can tweak your system or your services as you go, without having to commit to a long haul with a lot of people. Private coaching also allows you to really get your hands on people and enact big change, which also builds great case studies and testimonials!

—> *It's always popular with clients.* Trends in industries come and go, but there is a subset of people who always are going to want one-on-one support and service.

—> *It's one of the easiest ways to sell coaching.* How many emails have you ignored in your life?

If you are like most people, you don't read 60-80% of your email.

That means that when someone is selling coaching products or services over email to tons of people, you most likely aren't 1) seeing it or 2) opening it. But when you sell one-on-one coaching, you are often selling in-person, standing in front of someone or speaking to them over the phone. It's hard to ignore, and it's easy for you to have a real, authentic conversation with potential clients about how you can help.

The cons of private coaching

->*The biggest con of private coaching is that it isn't scalable.* What that means is that you are always trading time for money, and you only have so much time to give as a coach. Sure, you can keep raising your rates to make your time more profitable, but eventually, you will hit an upper limit on what you can charge, which means you will be limited on how much you can grow your business. For some people, this is 100% okay! You can make plenty of money coaching people one-on-one. For others, you may want more flexibility and room for growth. The great news? It's 100% up to you.

->*You have to stick to a reasonable schedule.* In my business, I love to be flexible. I like being able to be anywhere at any time, which I couldn't do when I had 6 client calls in a single day. I always had to make sure I was in the right time zone, at the right time. This is the tiniest violin complaint, but if you have a full caseload of clients (10-25), you will be on a regular routine. For you, that may be fabulous. For others, maybe not.

—> *You will need to have contracts.* For smaller and cheaper offerings, you can get away with a limited terms of service clause on your website that customers acknowledge at check out. But for services costing in the thousands, you will need to get a written contract in place with each and every client, so they understand your system and how it all works. While you can write a contract yourself, you will want to hire a lawyer to review it at some point to protect you (and your clients!).

Should you do it?
Yes.

Almost certainly yes.

It requires so little, in the beginning, to get going and get profitable, you can get clients with word-of-mouth marketing, and you can instantly get your business off the ground.

It's also a great way to test your system and get comfortable as a coach, all while building great testimonials that will serve you later.

You don't have to do private coaching for long, but it's a wonderful place to start!

The real money math

To start in private coaching, you can get a cheap or free website, and you don't need any other infrastructure besides a phone. With a bit of research, you can design a simple client contract on your own (though I recommend getting a legal eye on it as soon as possible).

So, let's do the math as an example of what you *could* make as a coach in full-time private practice.

If you close two clients per month at $2500 per package, that would = $5000 per month or $60,000 per year in gross income.

If you were to close four clients per month at $2500 per package, that would be $10,000 per month or $120,000 per year in gross income.

You'd subtract a small amount for operating fees like your online scheduler or website fees, but you'd easily spend less than $1500 a year in simple operations, meaning you get to keep almost all of it!

To reach that goal, you'd probably need to have a great, personal sales conversation with around 16 people per month, as you can expect to close around 25% of the people you speak within a sales consult or free coaching session.

If you are closing less than 25%, then something is wrong with how you sell your coaching, and if you are closing more, bravo!

How do you get started?

Getting started as a private coach is deceptively simple, but it does take some mental effort, so grab some coffee and put on your best thinking outfit!

1. **Figure out exactly, and specifically, who you are going to serve.** Get super clear on the demographics of your client *and* their big goal. You can't help everyone, so please stop trying. And specific does not include the words "clarity" "purpose" or "authentic." Instead, use words like "Senior manager team coach" "pregnancy-related grief coaching" or "Millennial promotion coach" - you get the idea!

2. **Set your coaching packages.** DO NOT CHARGE BY THE HOUR. It's bad business, and it's bad for client results. No coach can make a lasting life change in just an hour, it's just not possible. So, get your clients committed and engaged in the process by offering packages! Figure out how many sessions it'll take to get your client to their big goal, total it up, add in admin and other operational costs, and there's your package price (yay you!).

3. **Create a simple website** or LinkedIn Business page so people can find you. If you aren't ready for tech, a LinkedIn Business page is a good free way to start that has the simplest bar for entry.

4. **Start talking about your business, and how you help people.** Share your passion and begin to connect with real clients out in the world. Talk to friends, family, old co-workers, and new contacts to begin to spread the word. As you do, zero in on ONE marketing platform and stick to it. Don't try and be everywhere at once, so stop being on 5 social media platforms and running yourself ragged. Yes, I'm looking at you! *wink*

5. **See how all of this feels!** You may like it, you may not. It's important to stop during the business building process and assess how you are feeling about doing the operational stuff. Being in business as a solo-entrepreneur isn't for everyone, and that's okay! It's normal to have some anxiety and stress as you learn all of these new skills but assess if you are feeling stressed-but-excited, or stressed-and-unhappy. If it's the former, please keep going! If it's the latter, be kind to yourself for stepping outside of your comfort zone and trying anyway.

6. **Get your coaching system and contracts in place**. Once you start getting the word out, you can then figure out how you will onboard new clients and all the logistics that go with that (how will they get access to you? What days will you coach? What is your refund policy?).

7. **Then register your business and worry about your logo.** That stuff doesn't matter if you don't have a good process in place or if you are just "figuring things out."

Psst: If you want incredible practical details on how to get started, there's a free guide on how to start a private coaching business here: www.coachpony.com. You are welcome to grab it!

Tools you may need:
1. A website tool like **Wordpress** or business page on **LinkedIn**.
2. Payment tool like **PayPal** (or you can take checks in the beginning).
3. Email.
4. Word or Pages to take notes/create homework or worksheets.
5. Google calendar for internal scheduling and planning.
6. Calendar tool like **Acuity** or **Schedule Once,** to add a level of professionalism to your

coaching, and make scheduling clients and potential clients easier!

The short and dirty inside look:
I, like most coaches, started with private coaching as my very first money path.

I was scared, overwhelmed, and pretty sure I was going to fail, but I spent time and money in learning about how to structure and sell coaching, and then set my prices and hung out my shingle as a career coach for smart women who want to find their passion.

I charged my very first client $2000 for a 10-session package to help her find her career passion, and I quickly realized that the level of effort and access I was offering meant that I needed to up my rates.

So, I upped my rates to $2,500, and then $3500, and then I finally created a special VIP package for $5000.

It felt AMAZING when I got my first VIP client, and after dancing around the room I popped the champagne because I realized that I had started to figure *it* out.

By "it," I mean sales funnels, or how to create predictable income for your business.

Everything came together for me when I figured out that the marketing method I was best at was not social media or SEO or anything like that, instead it was speaking. So I spoke OFTEN. Everywhere that would have me, whenever I could I would offer to speak for free.

And each time I gave a speech I offered everyone in the room a chance to sign up for my introductory coaching package at a discount.

Using that package as my sales funnel, I got interested folks to agree to work with me more closely and sign up for one of my 10 session packages, either at the regular level or the VIP level.

I learned that as long as I spoke once a month, I could keep my coaching pipeline full of clients, and most excitingly, have a real life again because I knew I'd keep making money.

No more panicking over buying a cup of coffee! Nope, instead, I was ordering coffee AND muffins with abandon! (I kid, obviously I was eating cookies *wink*).

But my point is, *that* is how I started to make a real profit and got to my first six-figures in business all those years ago!

Note: I still run that career coaching business, and you can find it here if you are curious about what I offer and how I do it: www. therevolutionaryclub.com

And if you need to learn the business side of coaching like I did, I highly recommend you sign yourself up for this super-structured program here: www.buildarealbusiness.biz.

OPTION 2: GROUP COACHING

I love group coaching, it's so *much* fun. My group programs are the backbone of my coaching business for two reasons: Income and heart.

My first big group coaching program was how I reached multiple six figures early in my business (and even more now), and it's also where my heart still remains today. These programs fuel me in a special way because there's something magical to me about working with a group.

But the truth is that group coaching is not for everyone, and that's okay!

So, let's talk about what group coaching is, in this context: Group coaching is similar to private coaching, in that you are using a coaching process and working with people. It has a live component to it, whether it's literally meeting in-person in a group format, or on a live webinar or telecall with the group that you are serving.

It can also have formal training or teaching materials included, and it can include a live start and end date. Finally, a group program caters to a group of people over a period of weeks or months.

The big obvious difference between group and private coaching is that you are serving a group instead of individuals, and because of that the cost per person is lower.

Group program pricing can range quite a bit, so this one is hard to quantify. Many group programs start at the $200 price point, with an average around $500-$1000, topping out at around $2000 per person.

The pros of group coaching:
–>*Group coaching, unlike private coaching, is 100% scalable.* Meaning, once you have developed your system and your method of delivery (phone, webinar, live workshop etc), you can add additional people to your program with little to no extra effort. My group programs are designed to have hundreds of people participate all at once, which means that I have dramatically leveraged my time and my reach.

However, not every group program can scale to hundreds or thousands. Scaling depends on how much contact you want to have with everyone in your group cohort, and how personal you want the experience to be.

But it is scalable, and that's why it's an effective business model.

–>*Community adds to the experience.* While there is a lot to be said for one-on-one support, people learn SO MUCH from each other. In a group setting, I've found that better questions are asked, clients can get support and validation from each other, and there's a sense of belonging that contributes to your students making great progress.

Some people also love to lurk, are shy, or are scared to ask questions. They can get so much learning from watching you coach others, or hearing questions asked by other clients.

Group coaching can also make you a better teacher and coach, as you field more and varied questions, and have people with different experiences interacting together.

–>*There's a lot of flexibility in group coaching.* I only offer group coaching programs at certain times of the year. What's nice about that is that I can take downtime in between and not be beholden to clients, and I can also deliver the programs from anywhere, as long as I keep time zones in mind when I plan my travels.

Tools like Facebook have made group coaching communities instantly accessible at any time, so I can have folks all over the world participate in my group programs and get feedback when they need it.

—>*Group coaching can help you avoid "repeat burnout."* If you end up coaching privately for a long time, you realize that most people go through the exact same set of issues to get to that goal that you help them achieve. After a while, you can get tired of explaining the same thing, or coaching on the same thing, again and again, *and again.*

By doing it in a group you reach more people and only have to explain or coach once which can help you avoid burnout in certain areas of your business.

—> *Group coaching is often offered at a lower price point, which means more people can get access to you.* You should be charging in the thousands (or AT LEAST $1000) for your private coaching package. But group coaching can be much cheaper for the individual, which makes it easier to say yes, and allows people from more walks of life access to coaching. Group programs can range from $97 per person to $2000 per person, but many are under $1000 which makes it *slightly* easier on the pocketbook.

The cons of group coaching

—>*Group programs often take much more effort to market and sell.* Private coaching practices can be built on referral and word of mouth. Landing one high-end private coaching client can pay for all of your monthly expenses, which can be a giant relief, especially in the beginning! But most group coaching can't come at the same premium price, so you need more people to enroll in your programs to make up the difference in price. That means a LOT more marketing and selling has to happen to fill your programs. That takes time and effort, and a whole separate skill set that you have to learn (or hire).

—>*Large programs require more infrastructure.* The truth is that my first group coaching program relied solely on freeconferencecall.com and my personal yahoo email address (I know!!) to send out the homework to my students. But, as the program grew from 5 people to 500, and the price increased from $197 to $1200, I had to put so much more in place for the program. Now my group programs have private portals, big email campaigns, ad budgets, IT support people, community managers and all the bells and whistles. This infrastructure took me years to develop and build – in addition to revamping the program and delivering it as well. That takes time, and it's both frustrating and tiring.

–>*In the beginning, group programs can fail.* What if you create a snazzy new program that you are all excited about, you pour time and resources into it, and only a handful of people sign up? Then you are stuck delivering a program to too few people for too little cash. It can feel soul-destroying, especially when you are first starting out and you don't have a cash safety net. So many new coaches immediately want to build and deliver a great group program, but they forget to take into account how much goes into building, selling and marketing these programs to make them worthwhile to run. So, while I LOVE them, don't think that they are easy or fast – to do right, they take both time and effort.

–> *The industry is changing.* There are a LOT of people out there who will tell you that group or online programs are going to change your life and business, and you need to do one NOW because 6-figures blah blah blah. But I'm here to tell you the truth: Things are changing in the coaching industry, and big, expensive live/online programs are not as popular with clients as they once were. I've interviewed tons of coaches who have experienced this shift and also seen changes in my own business that tell me that these programs might not be the reliable money-makers they once were, or even how people want to get their information or learning these days.

Should you do it?
Maybe.

As I said at the beginning of this section, group coaching isn't for everyone and that's okay!

To be successful running group programs, you need to be incredibly comfortable in marketing yourself and your services, and you need to be willing to put yourself out there (and face more rejection) than you would as simply a private coach.

You'll have programs that won't fill up, or won't sell out, and you need to be prepared for more ups and downs. If you can't hack the roller coaster and the almost certain fact that one of your programs will tank, then don't do it.

BUT, group programs are also amazing! It's a wonderful feeling to create a great community, extend your reach, and help more people. So, if you are okay with the added stress of marketing and launching a group program, they may be perfect for you.

The real money math

Let's take a look at the numbers, shall we?

To start in group coaching you will need a simple website and sales page, a free bridge line or a small webinar platform, and potentially the services of a designer to give your homework or handouts a little extra oomph.

As an estimate, that might cost you around $500-$1000 if you are super frugal.

Let's say you offer a group coaching program two times per year, and you limit it in size to 20 people. You charge $600 per person for 6 weeks of live group programming.

You would make $12,000 gross revenue per round of group coaching if you sell out.

Or, $24,000 per year with two rounds of offering.

If you charged $900 per person and had 30 people, you'd make $27,000 per round of coaching, and $54,000 per year...for 12 weeks of coaching work.

You'd probably have one or two refunds (which is normal), so plan on around $52,000 for the year. Still not bad!

To reach that number, you'd probably need to talk to at least 75-90 people each round one-on-one, going back to our 25% close rate on sales, and allowing for the fact that group coaching is cheaper so it *can be* easier to sell, though it still takes tremendous effort.

Or you would need to build an email community that is about 3,000 people strong if you are selling mostly via email. Why? Because you can expect only 1% of your email community to purchase your coaching. Numbers matter A LOT in sales.

How do you get started?
1. **Figure out the big transformation you will help your clients achieve.** After they've spent 4, 6, or even 10 weeks in your group program, what specifically will be different in their lives? Make sure this is something both concrete and that they actually want (versus something that you think that they need). This is not the time to use words like "abundance" or "clarity" as the big goal. People want specific things like a promotion or a new job, so get super clear on how your program will help them.

2. **Map out each coaching session that you need to make it to that goal.** Will you do live coaching? A mix of coaching and teaching? Will

you have pre-homework or do it all on the live sessions? Figure out your structure and high-level agenda for each session but leave room for flexibility so you can adapt to your group's needs.

3. **Plan your numbers.** How many people can you effectively help in a group setting? Based on that, how many people do you want to enroll? It's better to start smaller and give people a more tailored experience in the beginning. It'll save you both time and stress, and also allow you to produce better results (as you will be able to focus more on individuals).

4. **Plan your launch.** Group programs have a beginning, middle and end, so there is a definitive start date. Pick that date and then back up 2-3 months. That's how much time you need to begin to market the program and spread the word. How will you do that? One-on-one sales? Via building an email list? What's your approach?

5. **Pick out your technology.** How will you deliver the program? Via phone, webinar, video, Facebook Live, what? Don't be afraid to start simply in the beginning and build slowly. Tech shouldn't be a stumbling block for you, it's okay to use a phone line in the beginning if you need to.

6. **Write your sales page.** Group programs need some sort of sales page where you describe the curriculum and experience. It's time to put that together now. Include the big goal of the program, why they should trust you, what's included (in detail), any common questions they might have that would prevent them from signing up, and a way to contact you. You will also need to include a refund policy and any appropriate terms and conditions.

7. **Get conservative.** If you aren't selling 1-to-1 in your group program, that means that you can expect about 1% of the people who find you online and receive your emails about the program to sign up. If you are selling 1-to-1 to get people to join, you can expect at least 25% of people to join, maybe more. So, think about your reach and get conservative with your numbers. How many people will you need to reach to fill your program?

8. **Commit.** You've got to commit to delivering the program. Don't be wishy-washy about it, or you increase your chances of failure.

Tools you may need

1. A sales page or information page that you can build in **Wordpress** or **Ontrapages.**

2. A bridge line or webinar platform to allow you to meet in a group. Try **freeconferencecallHD. com** for a bridge line, or **zoom.com** or **webinarjam.com** for a webinar platform.
3. Pages or Word to design worksheets.
4. Keynote or PowerPoint to design slides or other visual teaching aids.
5. A payment method like **PayPal** or **Stripe**.
6. A Contact Management System like **Mailchimp** or **Ontraport**. In the very beginning, you could use personal email if you are dealing with a small group.

OPTION 3: RETREATS

On the one hand, I love retreats. After all, who *doesn't* want to get paid to take an awesome vacation and help people?

On the other hand, retreats can be a super special challenge for your business.

But before we get to all of that, let's clarify what we mean by "retreat."

A retreat is usually a small group of people (3-20) that you take to a special location for a few days of intense work.

They often include meals, and can also include hotel and other extras, like group bonding experiences or pampering.

On the surface, retreats seem like a no-brainer, and they do have some fabulous pros...

Pros of doing retreats

–>You get paid to take a vacation! But seriously, it's super fun to have your business support your travel and creativity, and *retreats hit both.*

–>You can really get your hands on people. I never wanted to full-time private coach long-term, but when I transitioned to group coaching, writing, and DIY programs, I missed the hands-on rush of working with people closely, which is why I offered career retreats once a year. Retreats are a great way to scratch that itch without exhausting you or requiring a long-term commitment to your clients.

–>They are fun and exciting – getting away can give you all sorts of new insights for your business (separate from your actual retreat content). In addition, a new location can be a balm to your soul as you take in new experiences and work with people in a different format.

–>You can have repeat clients come back year after year. Once you finish with private clients, you can offer them a chance to come to your retreat each year for a check in or top up, or just a great experience. Done right, this can make them easier to sell over time.

Cons of doing retreats

->*I cannot state this enough: Retreats are often the LEAST PROFITABLE part of your business.* The reason? They require the most up-front costs. From renting a conference room (or house), providing food or other extras, to your own travel and expenses, things add up quickly. It's very easy to lose money on retreats, or not make any money at all once you tally up everything you've spent. Given that they take a lot of time to plan and deliver – this is less than ideal.

->*They take a massive effort to sell in the beginning.* But seriously – they are more difficult to sell because potential clients have two levels of buying pain to go through: 1) The pain of buying the retreat ticket and 2) The pain of buying airfare and/or hotel rooms. This "double pain" often stops people from signing up.

->*They require a LONG lead time.* If you want to sell a retreat and have a hope of filling it, you'll need to start selling it months in advance and allow for at least two big sales pushes, one at the beginning of your sales cycle, and one near the end. You've seen October conferences that start selling tickets in March, right? This is why. And those months of selling can be *exhausting.* Some people can commit early, but some can't till the last minute, you'll have to account for both. While you are doing that, it takes energy from the rest of your business.

–>*They can make you look bad.* What if you plan a retreat, sign a contract, and only sell 2 of 20 spaces? What do you do? Cancel? Hold a retreat for 2 people after you promised a community of 20? There's a lot of risk in running a retreat because you don't know if you will fill it or not, especially if your business is new and you are just building your community. Remember to always have a plan in mind for the worst-case scenario if you are thinking about running a retreat BEFORE you sign any contracts or crack open that bottle of champagne.

Should you do it?
Probably not.

Retreats are much easier to plan and pull off when you already have a raving fan base and a solid handle on your business.

As a new coach, the level of effort involved, difficulty, and risk makes them a tough choice, so I'd recommend saving them until you are an experienced business owner with a core base of clients.

The real money math
Retreats are tough for money math, because they have

so many different kinds of expenses, and many are optional and vary by location. It's therefore hard to quantify how much they might cost you, or how much money they might bring in.

But, let's take a crack anyway! As a rule of thumb, you can expect to spend at least 25-50% of your revenue on sunk costs, like your hotel room, travel, the venue, meals, materials, AV support, and other assorted costs.

So, if you offer a retreat for 5 people, and charge $4,000 per-person including 3 nights in a hotel and all meals, you would make $20,000 in gross revenue, and *might* spend $8,000+ on costs, meaning you will bring home $12,000 or less in profit per retreat.

If you did three retreats a year at the above rates and sold them all out (which is high, given how long they take to sell), you'd bring home around $36,000 in profit per year, plus you'd get three fun trips!

How do you get started?
1. **Set a goal or outcome of the retreat.** What will your clients walk out having completed? How will they feel at the end?

2. **Design the high-level agenda that will meet that goal.** How many days do you need

to reach that goal? (Hint: Two to four days is about right. Less makes it not worth the trip, more makes it too difficult to get away).

3. **Review venues and get pricing.** It's important to put together a solid budget projection for retreats. So, make sure you talk to different hotels and venues and get ideas on what things costs, remembering that prices vary greatly by both location and season. Review all the costs before you decide what you will include in the price of the ticket (and what you won't).

4. **Plan your double-launch.** How will you sell the retreat early on? How will you sell the retreat late in the game? What is your refund or backup plan if no one, or too few people, signs up?

5. **Set the date and start launch phase 1.** Remember, you want to start advertising the retreat months ahead of time.

6. **Plan the second push closer to the final enrollment period.** You'll need a second big push when the retreat date gets closer to get folks who couldn't commit earlier into your retreat. Make sure you have a second big marketing push scheduled to get their attention.

7. **Get help**. You will most likely need a second person for logistics, to handle anything weird that comes up during the retreat. A spouse, friend, task-rabbit, anyone who can be on standby to help you will be a huge part of the retreat success!

Tools you may need:

1. Website page or pdf handout that details what's included in the retreat. Retreats are one area where you don't have to have a sales page if you have a beautiful pdf document that you can share with your potential clients.
2. Excel spreadsheet for budget tracking.
3. Event or logistics coordinator to help you plan.
4. **Paypal** or **Stripe**, or another method of payment. You can also take a check, but if you are doing retreats you need to have a credit card option and be prepared to offer a payment plan.
5. Pages or word to design retreat materials.
6. A designer to help you create lovely branded materials for your retreat.
7. Email...of course! :)

The short and dirty inside look:

My first retreat was a total disaster. I decided randomly to do it with no real plan, found a place in Costa Rica because I wanted to take a vacation there, and threw up a small web page with limited information, but a whole lot of fun pictures of parrots.

You can already tell that this is going to end well, can't you?

I also did not think about the concrete outcomes I was offering besides the idea to "take your career on vacation" and "deep dive into your passion" ... neither of which is specific enough for people to pony up money to attend. That seems obvious now and you should be rolling your eyes at me, but in my eagerness to get away I didn't see it at the time.

So, not surprisingly, I had very little, i.e. zero, interest in my parrot-filled Costa Rica retreat. I lost the $500 deposit on the hotel when I had to cancel, and chalked it all up to a very big lesson learned.

I waited over a year before planning another retreat, but this time I had a much different approach: I prepared a beautiful designer-made pdf outlining everything attendees could expect on the retreat. I detailed the overall luxury experience, as well as the specific results that they could expect to take home. I created a list of people I knew would benefit from attending, and I put together a second, backup marketing plan built around guest blogging to help me fill the retreat if my first contact list failed.

That retreat was an unqualified success. We held it in Sonoma California, and filled every slot but one. We had such an amazing time... and even managed to stay tens of thousands of dollars in the black, which was a relief after my first disaster retreat ended up $500 in the red. It was everything I hoped it would be, and I got a very fun vacation out of it as well.

(Have I mentioned that I like wine?).

OPTION 4: WRITING A BOOK

It's fantastic when you can codify your expertise as a coach and create passive income that fuels your business and life, all at once.

Who doesn't love waking up to new sales, or helping people while you sleep? (True story: I once woke up to over $2000 of random book sales while I was on vacation in Europe. I don't like to be the kind of business coach who starts any kind of sentence with "while I was in Europe" because there's enough sleaze out there, but it was an amazing feeling, so skip the Europe part and just focus on making money while you sleep. Also, this is an insanely long tangent - my apologies!).

Long story short: Writing a book is a great way to create some passive income while you also cement your coaching knowledge and life experience.

Books are also great tools to help people get to know you and enter into your coaching world, ultimately to become a client in another one of your programs, or *book* you into a speaking engagement.

So, let's take a deeper look!

Pros of a book

—>*Having a low-cost item is great for your sales funnel.* Having a low-cost item is an easy way for people to get to know your approach and try you out before investing in something more expensive like private coaching or a retreat. If they like you, they are much more willing to invest!

—>*Writing a book gives you credibility,* you can literally say "I wrote the book on that!"

—>*Writing a book can help you codify what you teach and make you a better coach.* Nothing sharpens your process like writing it down, and really thinking through how you do things, why you do them, and most importantly, why they work. Thinking through how to teach your coaching system and creating this kind of content makes you go even deeper into your own learning, which can only help your skills as a coach.

—>*Writing a book allows you to help more people.* Not everyone can afford to spend hundreds or thousands of dollars on private or group coaching, but most people can afford to spend $10 on a book. This allows you to help more people to make big changes in their lives, and that's definitely work worth doing.

—>*They keep making you money.* Once you've written the book, you can sell it over and over again. And that's super fun.

Cons of a book
—>*They take a lot of time and effort to create.* Even if you are a fast writer, it takes time to map out your book, write it, edit it, format it, and research the best way to launch it (Amazon? Through your website? Traditional publishing routes?).

—>*You'll need to get help to get it designed and formatted.* You'll probably want to pay someone to design a cover and format your book for the distributor if you are self-publishing, which is the easiest way to go. You can spend a few dollars on Fiverr, or more on another platform like Upwork or 99 Designs. Amazon also offers free options for print and kindle as well, and if you have a design eye, you can design a cover for your book and format it there fairly easily.

—>*It takes a while to produce tons of income off of a book, and you might never make more than a few dollars a month.* Unless you are an amazing marketer (in which case, BRAVO!), or you have a book deal with a large advance, it'll be tough to make a living off of just a $5 or $10 self-published book. For most coaches, a book isn't the main source of income, it's a way to market their services and establish credibility.

Should you do it?
Maybe.

If you don't like writing and don't have a blog, starting with a book is not a good idea. There are plenty of other ways to market your business and make a living without adding a big project like this to your plate.

However, if you love writing as your main marketing platform, then a book *could* be a great idea, depending on your strategy. So, your first step is to start thinking about the real purpose behind writing your book. Is the book just a form of credibility? Is it a way to market your business? Is it the first step of a bigger sales funnel? What is the purpose of the book?

No matter what your bigger strategy, books become easier to produce if you have a blog that can serve as some of the material for your book, and if you also already have a proven coaching method or system that you can share as the backbone structure to your writing.

Struggling with creating your coaching system? Here's an in-depth resource to help you: www. buildarealbusiness.biz

The real money math
Let's say you self-publish a book on Amazon and on your website and price it at $10.

If you sell 50 of them a month, you've created an income of $500 per month, or $6000 a year.

To sell 50, you'd need to reach 2500-5000 people per month of potential buyers, going back to our 1% rule of thumb for online sales. Because you'd have the power of a search engine like Amazon directing interested people to your work, I'm bumping it up to 2%.

If you have a bigger coaching program and you create a sales funnel using your book, you might conservatively sell 50- 100 books per month. Of those 50 -100 people, you might have one or two people buy your $2000 coaching program after reading the book and getting nudged via email into a sales funnel to buy the bigger program.

That means that you'd make $24,000 - $48,000 gross revenue in terms of your program, plus an additional $6,000 - $12,000 per year in straight book sales.

That would mean a total gross revenue of $30,000 - $60,000 per year if you choose to use your book as a marketing tool for a bigger program.

How do you get started?

1. **Decide the theme and overall vision for your book.** What are you teaching and why is it important?

2. **Decide your strategy.** How will you use your book in your business? Is it a form of credibility to help you get speaking engagements? Is it a marketing tool to drive people to your community to purchase more expensive programs? If so, what is your sales funnel to get speaking engagements or to drive people into your program funnel?

3. **Review any blogs or articles you've written, and ask yourself:** Can any of them be repurposed for the book?

4. **Set aside time to write each day** and add it to your calendar. Even 30 minutes a day can go a long way to helping you complete a book in 4 or 8 weeks.

5. **Plan how you want to sell your book.** Will you sell it on your website? From Amazon or another provider? Will you do both?

6. **Hire someone to help you with the formatting design and cover.** Make sure this looks reasonably professional.

7. **Let people know your book is coming.** Consider releasing chapters to friends and family ahead of time, to get feedback or create buzz.

8. **Plan a marketing strategy for the launch of your book when it's *almost* ready.** Will you do a promo on Amazon where you offer the book for free or very little? Will you do a launch to your community? Will you host an event? Will you go on podcasts or write articles to promote it?

9. **Launch!**

Tools you may need:

1. A simple landing page to generate interest for the book before you release it **(Leadpages** or **Ontrapages**).

2. Word or pages for writing the book.

3. Designer from **Fiverr** or **Upwork** or another design service to create your cover (Amazon has some simple free options as well).

4. Copy-editor (friend or family member, or a professional copy editor).

5. A timer like **tomato-timer.com** to help you focus and write in chunks, just in case you have writer's block :).

6. A marketing platform like **Amazon, Facebook,** or your own website and email community.

OPTION 5:
CREATE A DIY ONLINE PROGRAM

Online programs are amazing, they are another great way to help people while you are asleep, which is a wonderful feeling.

I love knowing that I'm helping people in their careers and businesses while I'm not even there! It makes me feel like Batman. If only I had an Alfred, then my bat suit, i.e. sweatpants, might not be so wrinkled.

But ANYWAY, when I talk about a DIY online program, I'm referring to a program that is often resident online, it usually involves video or audio recordings, and does not involve a real-time live component like a group call or webinar.

Once it is sold the delivery is 100% automated, meaning that you do not participate in the delivery of the program and it happens seamlessly and automatically over email and through your tech systems.

The program can be something that people get access to all at once or dripped out over a period of weeks.

These programs are often called "evergreen" meaning that they are always available and accessible, and a customer can buy it and begin the program at any time.

Evergreen DIY programs are normally priced under $500, often in the $50-$200 range.

Pros of an online DIY program
—>*They are evergreen and can make money all year.* It's wonderful to wake up to money in your bank account and know you are helping people while you sleep. That gives you a freedom in your life that you might not have had otherwise. Yay!

—>*They are infinitely scalable.* There's no involvement of your time on delivery of the program, so hundreds or thousands of people can sign up!

—>*They are very profitable.* There are some upfront costs and learning associated with building an online DIY program, from building a website to creating nice materials. However, once you've done it you can keep reselling the program and making money without having to continue to make major investments. It's a very profitable system.

—>*They are helpful if you want major flexibility in your business.* Not being beholden to having specific hours of coaching or teaching, like you would in private coaching or group coaching, means you have a huge amount of flexibility in your business. It's much easier to travel or work odd hours if no one is scheduling meetings to speak with you live.

Cons of an online DIY program
—>*They take time and effort to build.* You'll need to have a program that reflects well on your brand, from content to design. So, there will be an upfront cost of time and effort to get everything in place.

—>*They require some knowledge of tech.* You'll need a sales page, you'll most likely need to create videos, audios, in-depth worksheets, and all of the other bells and whistles that you'd expect if you bought an online program. Even if you start simply, you'll still need to master some technical programs, which can be a lot to learn all at once.

—> *They need infrastructure.* You'll need to sign up for a Contact Management System like Mailchimp or Ontraport in order to set up automated delivery of the product and learn the fun world of sequences, welcomes, customer support, refunds, payment, and sales pages. "Selling while asleep" only happens after a lot of learning and set up!

—>*They require regular marketing to maintain an income.* You'll have to have a solid launch and maintenance plan in place to ensure that your program consistently makes you money over time, to pay off for all of your initial up-front effort.

—>*You'll need to reach a lot of people to make a good income.* Marketing an evergreen program usually means that you are selling it via email and the internet, which means that only a small percentage of people who see it will buy it. To sell a lot of them, you'll need to reach a lot of people and have a very high-converting and polished sales funnel.

Should you do it?
Maybe.

This is an intermediate level of product offering because it requires a higher level of tech, infrastructure, and marketing to really work for your business.

If you enjoy all of the above, it could be a great money path for you to take once you get up and running.

I don't recommend it as your first step, however, because of the knowledge and skill involved to get started, plus the effort it takes to get traction on this product and make a real profit.

The real money math

Let's say you create an online program that costs $197. It consists of keynote or PowerPoint videos and lovely worksheets that you post on your website under password protection, plus email training delivered on a drip sequence spread out over three weeks.

That means that people buy your product, get a welcome email with a password, sign in to watch your content, and get emails with more information or prompts delivered automatically for the next three weeks.

If you sell 50 of them a month, you'll make $9850 per month or $118,200 per year as gross revenue.

If you factor in set up costs (probably $1500 - $3000) plus ongoing program costs (say $300 per month for your mail system and small extras) and refunds, you'll probably keep around $102,000 per year. This doesn't include marketing your program, which could be done mostly for free in the beginning but might also include paid ads.

To sell 50 programs per month, you'd need to get 5,000 people in your sales funnel...almost every month.

That's a lot of marketing!

How do you get started?
1. **Figure out what problem you are solving with your product**, and make sure that it's something people want!

2. **Think about the best form of delivery of your content**. Audio? Video? Writing? All of the above? What will best serve your clients?

3. **Plan out how your product will work based on your content delivery**, and begin to design the content. Create a clear content flow and process, so clients see that you are credible.

4. **Hire a designer to make everything pretty.** You definitely want people to feel like they are getting what they paid for, and a good design adds to the value.

5. **Get the tech sorted out.** You will need to set up a Contact Management System (CMS), sales page, website portal for the program itself, and sales funnel at a minimum. To help, you

will probably need to hire a developer at some point unless you are a person with a tech bent (go you!).

6. **Set your price.** It's okay to start cheap and raise the price as you learn, it's harder to set a price that's too high and not see good results.

7. **Set up your sequence of delivery and test it.** Get your systems in place, and make sure everything works. Sign up as if you were the client and go through the whole process.

8. **Figure out your sales funnel for this product, and test it.** How will you get people interested? What is their process to learn about the product or program? Email? Webinar? Ads? What is your sales funnel?

9. **Design your marketing plan.** How will you drive people to find you and your program? How will you hit your numbers target?

Tools that may be helpful:
1. Contact Management System like **Mailchimp** or **Ontraport**, to manage the email leads and delivery of the program.
2. Payment systems like **Paypal** or **Stripe**
3. Website or landing page for your sales page like

Wordpress or **Leadpages**

4. Website for the program itself like **Wordpress**, or an all-in-one system like **Teachable.**

5. A plugin to protect the Wordpress content like **Pilot Press** or **WishList Member**, or instead use an all-in-one system like **Teachable.**

6. Designer to make things look good, try **Upwork**.

The short and dirty inside look:

My book Zero to Passion was actually my first real online DIY program because I offered several tiers of learning.

(You can check it out here if you are curious as to what the different tiers of learning are: www. zerotopassion.com).

But my second was something I created called the Networking Masterclass. I knew that networking was a huge key skill related to careers and passion, and I wanted to test if my audience truly wanted more networking help.

So, I offered a paid webinar to my email community, called the Networking Masterclass, for a "pay what you can afford" rate with a recommended price of $59. At this point, I had thousands of people on my email list, and therefore I knew I'd get a response. But I wasn't sure if it would be a good one, so I did the barest minimum amount of effort to test this idea, meaning I only created a small checkout page and sent a few emails.

At this stage, I didn't even bother to create the webinar. I wanted to wait and see if anyone actually wanted to buy it *before* I spent time building it.

Once I alerted my community, I was proved happily correct. Before ever building the webinar I made $7,000 from my emails announcing the program. Since people could choose to pay as little as $5 for it I honestly wasn't expecting to make very much money, I just wanted to see if people would pay *anything*.

And...yes, yes they would! With that cash in hand, I knew I had a viable product.

Once the webinar was delivered (yes, I did create it as soon as I started getting payment!), I set about creating all of the bells and whistles of a true DIY online program, including a private portal that my developer built, lovely professional training videos, professionally designed slides and worksheets, and a variety of bonus material.

I offered the program for $197, and it sold really well for the first few days...and then...crickets!

I realized I had made a mistake with this money path because I hadn't set up a strong enough sales funnel to generate ongoing income.

Over the next few months, I tinkered with it and played with how I was marketing and offering the program, designing different sales funnels for it...and now it makes me anywhere from $1,000 - $14,000 every single month, which is fun for a program that's completely automated.

Not bad for something that started off as just a random idea, no?

OPTION 6:
BECOME AN AFFILIATE
OR REFERRAL PARTNER

Have you ever been so much in love with a business that you recommend them to friends?

That's the essence of being a good affiliate partner. I've partnered with different people and programs over the years, and it's always nice to get a random check in the mail for making a simple recommendation.

To get into the details: An affiliate is someone who markets a 3rd party program or service in exchange for a referral fee. Coaches are happy to pay partners because it means you get a great client with almost no up-front effort or marketing fees on your end.

When you are first starting out I highly recommend that you make friends with other coaches who have similar demographic audiences. Build a relationship with them and become referral partners with each other as a way to build your business AND help direct clients who *may* not be a fit for your personality or style to coaches who can better serve them. Everyone wins!

Pros of being an affiliate partner

–>*You don't have to have your own services taped out yet.* When you partner with someone you can start by marketing their services or products to people, while you work on your website or launching your own coaching practice.

–>*Sometimes it can be easier to sell someone else's stuff instead of your own.* Sales is a skill, so a way to sharpen your skill set in the beginning can be to try and market and sell for someone else. It feels less personal and scary because you don't have to sell *you*, and affiliate or partners will often have tips and support to help you learn how to sell their services.

–>*You don't have to have payment systems.* Affiliates often pay you by check or Paypal, so you don't have to have your own payment systems or infrastructure in place to start making money.

–>*It's something you might do anyway!* If you love the coach or product, there's a good chance you would recommend it or share it – so why not also get paid? It's a win-win! And to be clear, I think you should only partner with someone who you really like, who has a product or service you 100% believe in (i.e., you'd recommend it even if you weren't getting paid).

−>*It's a place for you to send clients you might not want to work with.* If you are private coaching you may run across people who aren't a good fit for your coaching services or personality, so having a referral partner on hand to send them to is a wonderful win. They get a great coach, you don't work with someone who isn't a fit, the other coach gets a new client and you get paid for your trouble. Everyone wins!

Cons of being an affiliate partner

−>*You have to be willing to sell.* You do have to have conversations, write up some emails, be willing to follow up, and put yourself out there if you want to make sales for your affiliate. So, there is some work involved if you want to get reasonable referral fees. Just posting on Facebook or sending out a blanket email isn't enough.

−>*Not every affiliate makes a great partner.* Some people aren't great to work with, they pay you late, or they don't do a great job of selling themselves so even when you send over great candidates they don't close the sale.

–>*It can be hard to make a lot of money.* Unless you already have a large community (and I'm guessing you don't since you are reading this), it may be hard for you to make tons of money as an affiliate. You may make several hundred dollars here, or a thousand there, but probably not enough to live on.

Should you do it?

Yes, with a caveat.

The caveat is that you should only affiliate or partner with someone you'd feel good about recommending for free.

Anytime you recommend someone, you are putting your own reputation on the line, so you want to make sure that you are protecting yourself and your clients.

But, if there is a program or service you love and you'd recommend, then, by all means, see if they have an affiliate or partner program!

There's no reason why you can't spread the word about something great and get paid at the same time :).

The real money math

This is probably the hardest money path to accurately predict the type of income you can earn, given that it is so wide-ranging, and everyone has a different payment formula for their affiliates.

As a rule of thumb, you can expect to make 25-50% of the client fee for your referral, depending on how much your partner's product costs. You'll make closer to 25% for private clients where the fee and labor is high, and nearer to 50% for products or services where the fee and labor might be lower.

But for fun, let's say that you partner with an affiliate who pays you $600 per referral. This number is an average of what I traditionally pay my affiliates.
You might refer 3 or 4 people to them per year, making your revenue close to $2400 per year. If you were aggressive and focused as an affiliate partner, you might refer 6-10 people per year, making your revenue between $4800-$6000 per year.

This is definitely NOT enough to live on, which is why becoming a partner should be a secondary source of income and not your primary money path. However, it's a great way to build your network, expand your portfolio when you can serve a particular client, and make a little money on the side.

How do you get started?

1. **Research other coaches who have similar demographics** in terms of their client base, or operate in the same niche as you do.

2. **Make a list of people who have programs that you would recommend for free** or have tried and loved.

3. **Reach out to both groups and see if they have public partnership programs posted on their websites**. If not, reach out with a personalized email offering to chat about partnering, making it clear that you are interested in helping them. Flattery also goes a long way!

4. **Hop on the phone and learn more!** Remember, only choose programs and partners you would wholeheartedly recommend for free. That keeps the sleaze out of being a partner!

Tools that are helpful:

Not to be cute but this is super simple:

1. Google, LinkedIn, and Pinterest for partner research.
2. Email and social media to reach out to partners.
3. Sincere flattery and appreciation always go a long way!

Final note: Don't forget taxes!

I've not taken taxes into account on any of these money paths because it's so hard to predict the amount of profit you may take home after expenses. However, it's a good rule of thumb to set aside 30% of your profit for taxes, that way you will never be surprised when it's time to pay up!

An Important Reminder + What's Next For YOU

Marketing matters.

Many new coaches get incredibly excited about being a life coach because they hear all of these wonderful stories about running a coaching business, and they assume that with enough excitement and positivity they can make it work.

They forget that building a business is an entirely different animal to being a coach.

And that each of these money paths requires a lot of marketing, to a lot of people, in order to make a real living.

So, remember to take a close look at the numbers I mentioned for marketing in each money path to get a dose of reality.

I don't want to throw cold water on your dreams.

Building a coaching business is NOT rocket science.

But it takes a lot of effort, knowledge, and know-how to get going and do well.

You can absolutely do it!

Just remember these numbers as you get out there and start promoting yourself as a coach, and don't get discouraged.

Most of the time if you feel like you are failing as an entrepreneur, it's not because you are a bad coach, *it's just because you haven't reached enough people yet.*

Final Thoughts to Help You + Free Resources

(You can do this!)

In some ways, this information may have seemed like a lot.

In some ways, you may have found yourself wanting more.

And, in some ways, you may still be wondering where you should go next.

So, let's tackle those three feelings:

1) If you found yourself a little overwhelmed by the information in this guide, please relax. You will figure it out.

Make sure you start simple and small in your business and take things one step at a time.

You don't have to tackle everything at once to be a success!

—>And if you are struggling with whether you should even BE a coach, please go here and take this free quiz to help you figure it out: www. coachpony.com/business-quiz.

2) If you found yourself wanting more, don't worry!

This isn't meant to be an exhaustive guide on how to successfully build a business in each of these paths - that would be a hefty tome that would take you weeks to get through.

I want this program to help focus your time and attention on the right money path for you. Once you know what that is, you can throw your whole heart and mind into mastering it!

And if you are thinking: "I really REALLY want more resources right now!" then I've got a free video series for you, it's all about the ins and outs on how to make money as a coach including a deep dive into choosing your niche and having real sales conversations!

—> Find it here: www.coachpony.com/free-training

3) If you are still wondering "what's next for me?" You aren't alone!

Being an entrepreneur is a marathon, not a sprint.

But I've found that every time I struggle or seem to hit a crossroads, as long as I take a deep breath and sit with my conflict for a few days, things will eventually become clear.

However, sitting does not mean staying still.

To figure things out *you must take action*. But it's okay to consciously meditate on your path and see what opportunities come your way while you find your way forward.

So, while you do that here's the specific action I want you to take right now: Go re-read the guide and eliminate the money paths that don't feel good to you, and then go back through and eliminate any that require too much up-front effort for you now.

That will be enough to get you on the road to clarity and let go of some of the weight of having too many choices.

Mostly, remember to keep it simple! Because honestly, there's great news that I want you to keep first and foremost in your mind:

Most of the money paths create enough money to live on right away, and several of them will allow you to reach six figures using *only* that path.

So, don't feel like you have to dive down multiple paths at once! Instead, pick one to start (my advice is to start with private coaching for all the reasons I listed in that option) and move forward from there.

You've got this.

YOU can do this.

Now get out there and make it happen!

But before you do, one more thing...

WAIT!!!
Grab your free training!

We've got two additional amazing free resources for you to help you make money as a coach because you deserve it!

1) Worried or anxious? Take our quiz to see if you are ready to start your business and be a coach, and then get access to free training designed to meet you exactly where you most need help!

—> Tap here on Kindle or go to this link: www. coachpony.com/business-quiz

2) Ready to start your business but need details on how to actually get paying clients? No problem! Here's a free, practical, in-depth video training on how to do the business side of coaching, so that you get REAL paying clients. We've got you covered!

—>Tap here on Kindle or go to this link to grab the free video training: www.coachpony.com/free-training

BONUS

And, if you want a free bonus training on how I sell coaching and built my business up from literally nothing - including some detailed examples that you are welcome to steal - then please write an honest review on Amazon and then email us admin@therevolutionaryclub.com letting us know you did.

We'll immediately send you the super-secret bonus training!

We trust you, no proof necessary.

"If you are walking down the right path and you're willing to keep walking, eventually you'll make progress." - Barack Obama

Why, Hello!

The official "About Christie/Coach Pony" statement:

Christie Mims is the founder of the Forbes Top 100 Website for Careers, The Revolutionary Club. Her work has been featured on Fast Company, Forbes, INC, Yahoo, US News, and a variety of other amazing places.

After spending years coaching people around their careers, Christie expanded her business to help new life coaches master the business side of coaching - because you can't help people if you don't have a business. And coaches deserve happy careers :).

That's when Coach Pony was born! It's time to saddle up and make your coaching dream a reality...people need YOU.

The unofficial statement:

Being a coach is amazing.

It's hard.

It's tiring.

It's fun.

It's creative.

It's maddening.

It's the best job on the planet.

But too many people (re: skeezy business coaches) are out there selling unicorns and rainbows.

You know what we need more of? Real truths. Honesty. What it's really like, including the good, bad, and ugly.

Sometimes you have chocolate on your pants.

Sometimes you do something you think is amazing, and it's a total flop.

Sometimes you just want to throw up your hands and give up.

But you don't - *because people need your help.*

So that's why Coach Pony exists - to be the honest place you can get business help and advice. A place where you can learn more about what it really takes to be a successful coach, and concrete steps on how to do it...for free.

—>Find us, and plenty of FREE resources here: www.coachpony.com

And if you are 100% ready to build your own money path as a coach, you can put your money where your mouth is and join the Build a REAL Business program. It's a real, concrete, chocolate-covered program designed to help you get happy, paying clients.

Because here's the other real truth: *If you aren't willing to invest in yourself and your learning, why should you expect your clients to do the same?*

Curious? Learn more about Build a REAL Business (the step-by-step business training focused solely on coaches), and get access to testimonials and case studies right over here!

You don't have to go it alone. We can help carry you and your business forward. That's why we are Coach Pony, after all!

Mostly, welcome to our world. You deserve to be here. YOU are amazing!

The best business training for new coaches is right here —> go and get it! www.buildarealbusiness.biz

Printed in Great Britain
by Amazon